TASTY TUNES

10 ORIGINAL PIANO PIECES BY WENDY STEVENS

ISBN 978-1-4803-5385-5

EXCLUSIVELY DISTRIBUTED BY

WILLIS MUSIC

HAL•LEONARD®
CORPORATION
7777 W. BLUEMOUND RD. P.O. BOX 13819
MILWAUKEE, WISCONSIN 53213

Visit Hal Leonard Online at
www.halleonard.com

From the composer

When I was a kid, I remember spending hot afternoons sitting in the grass beside my house drinking cold pickle juice from a plastic cup. If you think that sounds like an interesting idea, then you're probably a kid who already knows that foods are just plain fun! So whether you like eating pickle sandwiches, mixing your fries with your ice cream, biting lemons, or enjoying ice cream on a Sunday afternoon, I hope you have a fun time with these crazy, tasty tunes!

Wendy Stevens

P.S. I'd love to hear about your favorite food combos! You can email me on my website **www.composecreate.com** or on my Facebook page: **www.facebook.com/ComposeCreate**.

CONTENTS

Macaroni Pizza

Words and Music by
Wendy Stevens

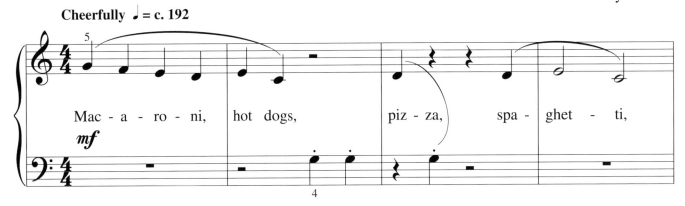

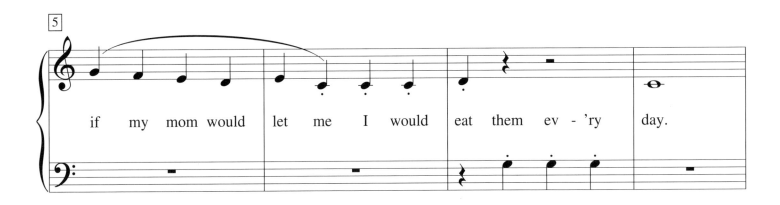

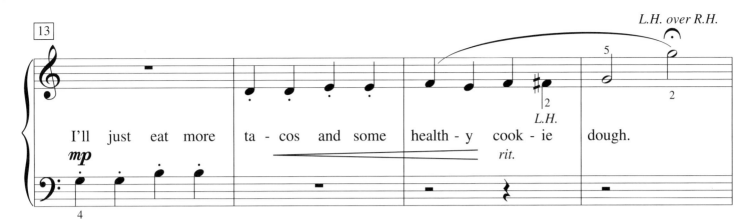

I'll just eat more ta - cos and some health - y cook - ie dough.

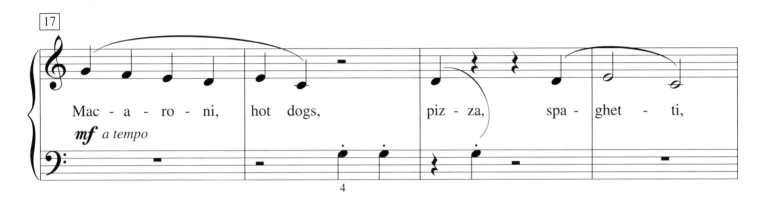

Mac - a - ro - ni, hot dogs, piz - za, spa - ghet - ti,

if my mom would let me I would eat them, eat them,

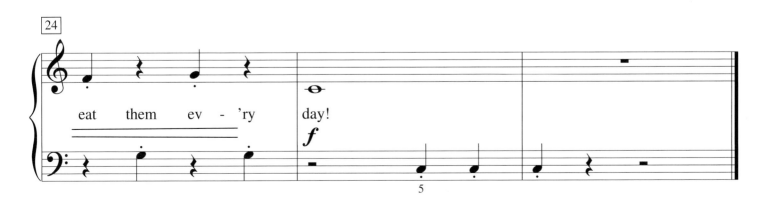

eat them ev - 'ry day!

Take Off the Peel

Traditional Irish Jig
Lyric by Wendy Stevens

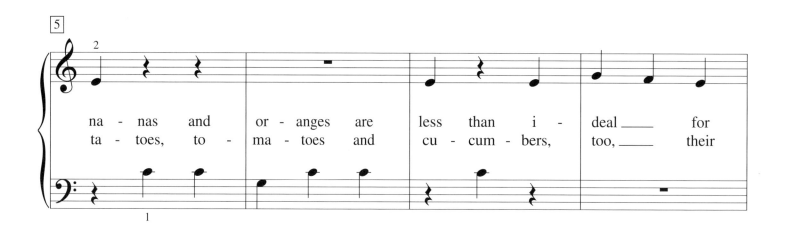

na - nas and or - anges are less than i - deal ___ for
ta - toes, to - ma - toes and cu - cum - bers, too, ___ their

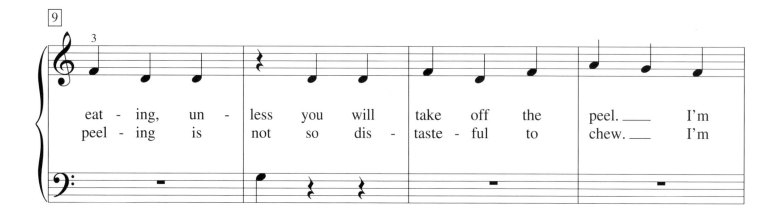

eat - ing, un - less you will take off the peel. ___ I'm
peel - ing is not so dis - taste - ful to chew. ___ I'm

sure they won't | hurt me, but | let's make a | deal: ___ I
sure if you | try them you'll | like - ly con - | strue: ___ a

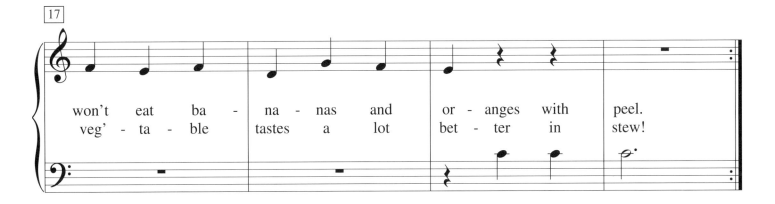

won't eat ba - | na - nas and | or - anges with | peel.
veg' - ta - ble | tastes a lot | bet - ter in | stew!

CODA

French Fries, Ice Cream

Words and Music by
Wendy Stevens

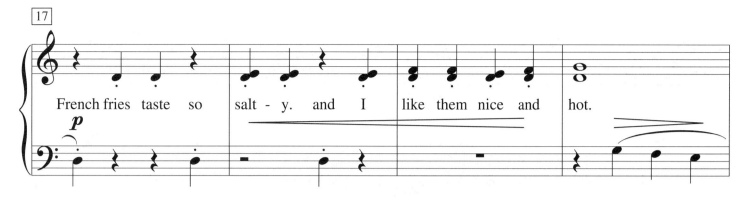

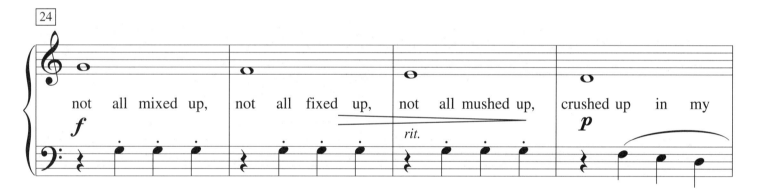

A Pickle Sandwich

Words and Music by
Wendy Stevens

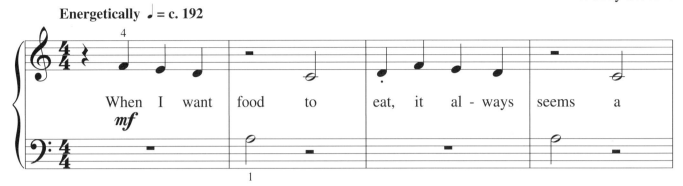

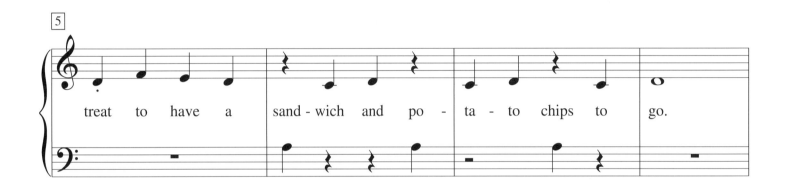

When I want food to eat, it al - ways seems a

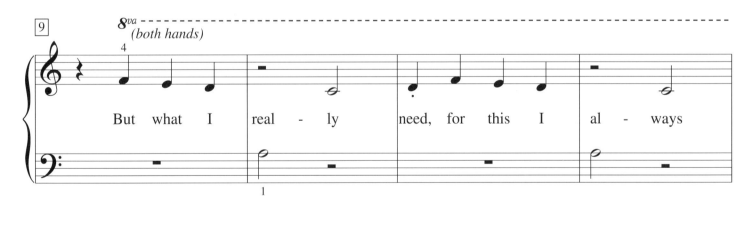

treat to have a sand - wich and po - ta - to chips to go.

But what I real - ly need, for this I al - ways

plead: a food that Mom can't un - der - stand or e - ven know!

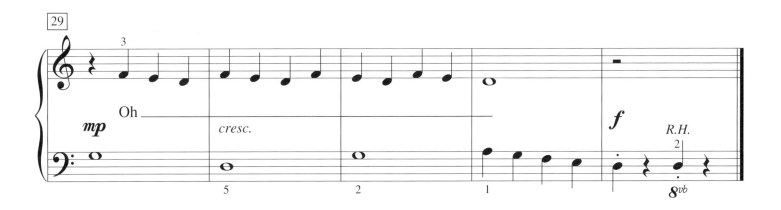

Crazy for Lemons

Words and Music by
Wendy Stevens

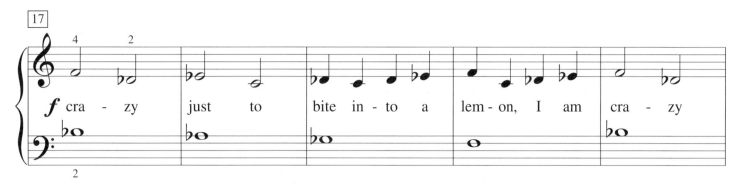

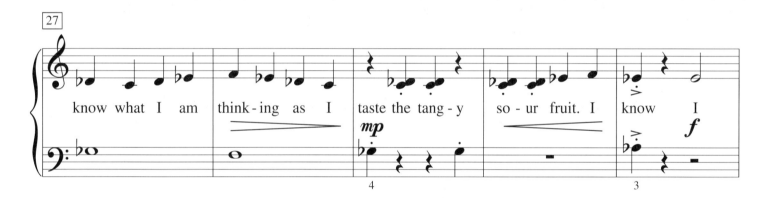

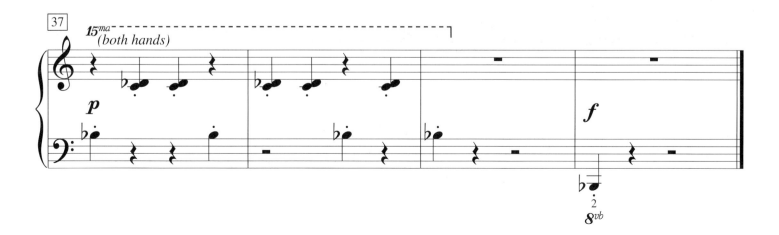

A Nice Exotic Blend

Try filling in your own crazy food combos
the 2nd time you play the chorus.

Words and Music by
Wendy Stevens

Some folks like their food in sep-'rate plac - es

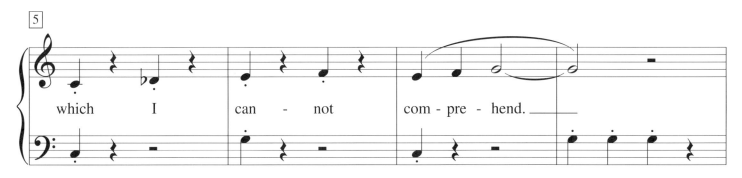

which I can - not com - pre - hend.

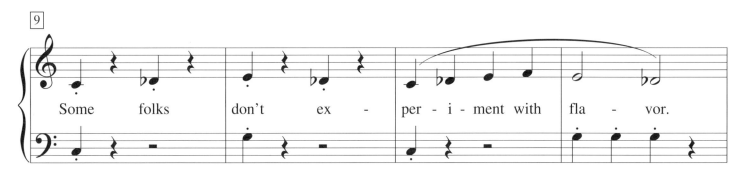

Some folks don't ex - per - i - ment with fla - vor.

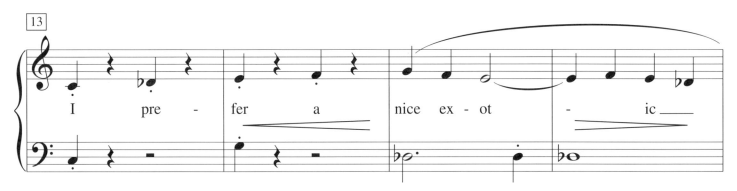

I pre - fer a nice ex - ot - ic

blend.

15

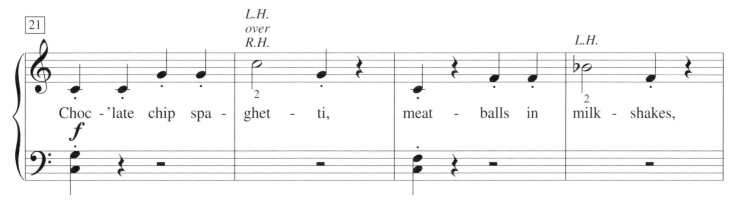

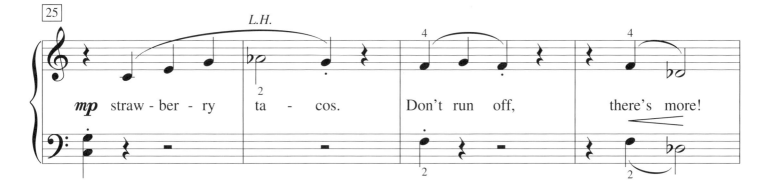

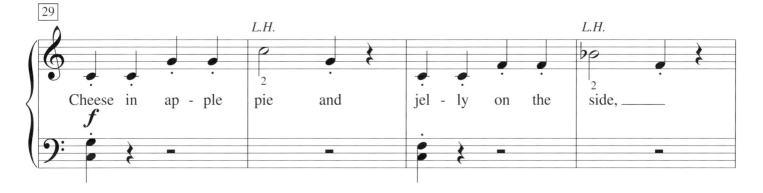

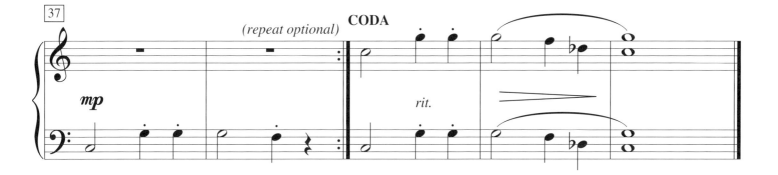

Ice Cream on a Sunday Afternoon

Wendy Stevens

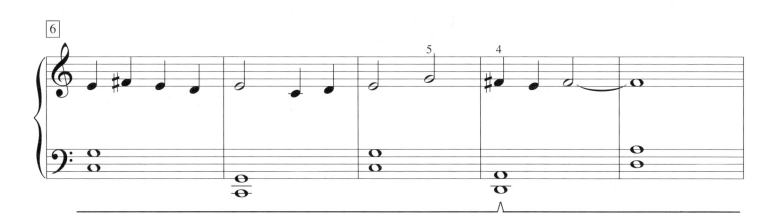

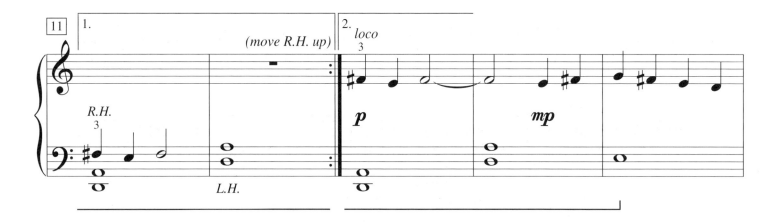

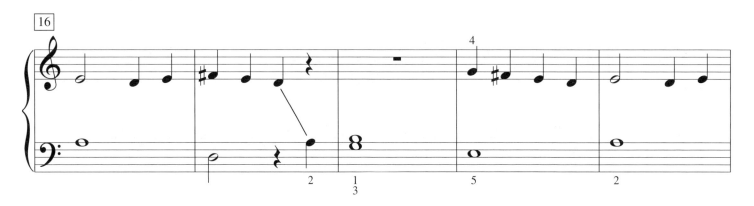

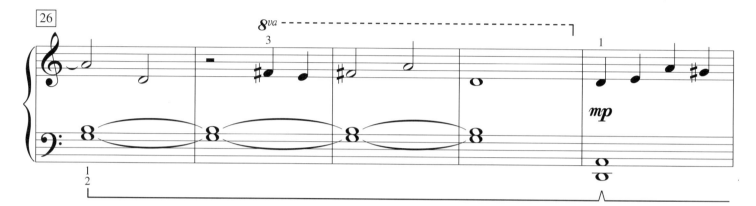

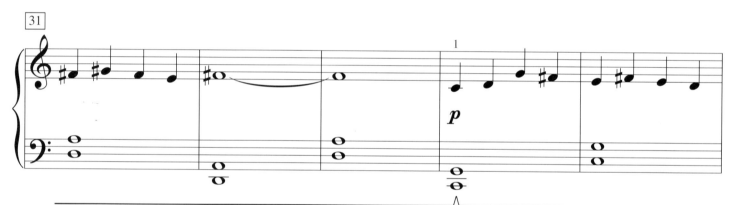

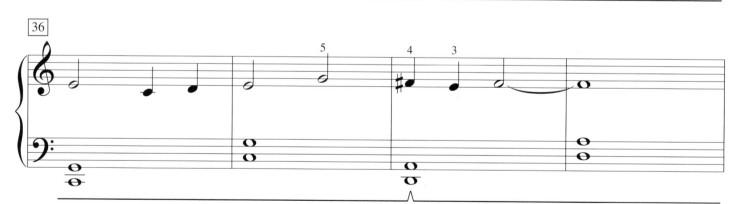

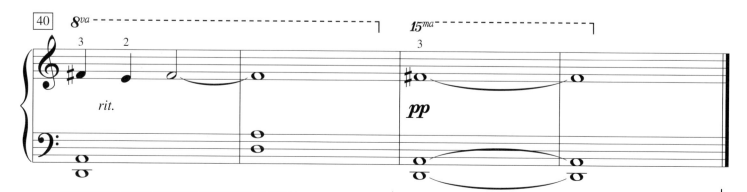

I Love My Ranch

Words and Music by
Wendy Stevens

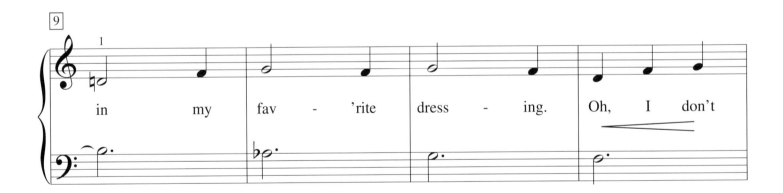

(Move R.H. up)

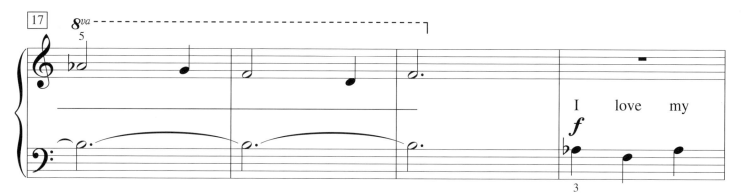

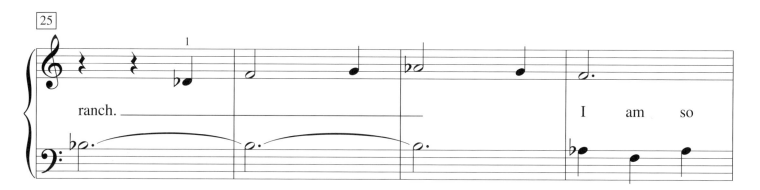

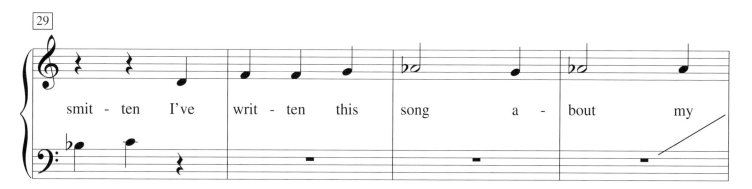

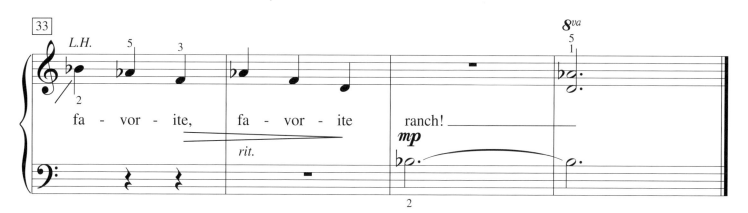

Angel Food Cake

Wendy Stevens

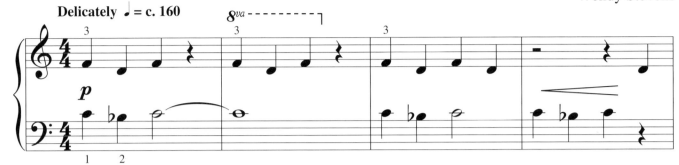

Hold pedal down throughout

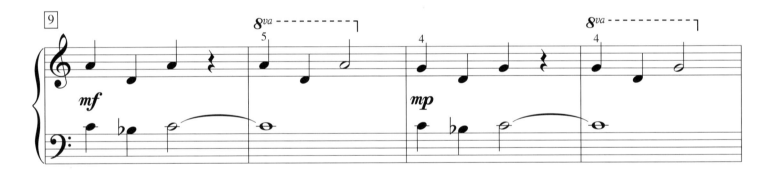

Rock 'n' Roll Rotini

Words and Music by
Wendy Stevens

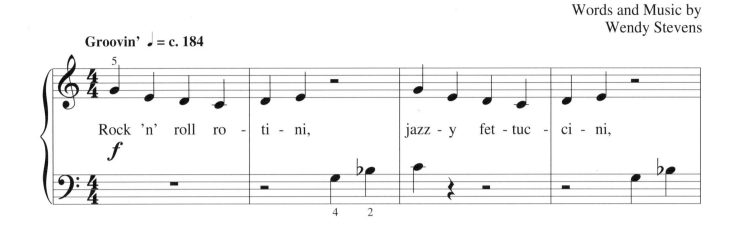

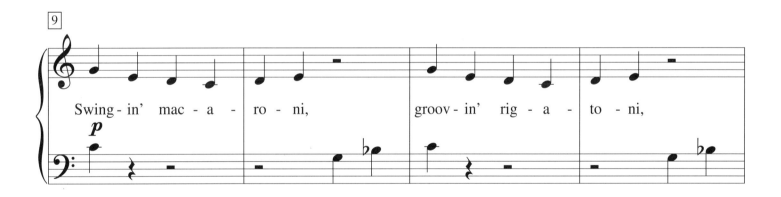

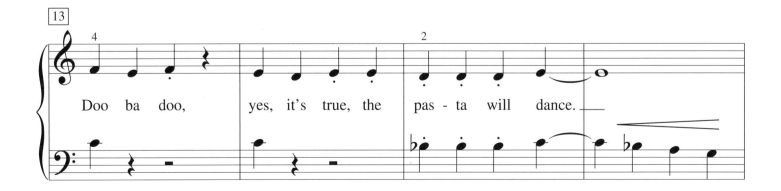

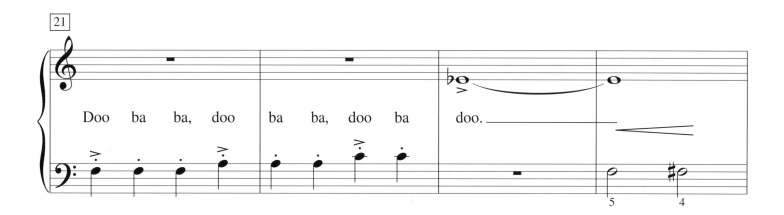

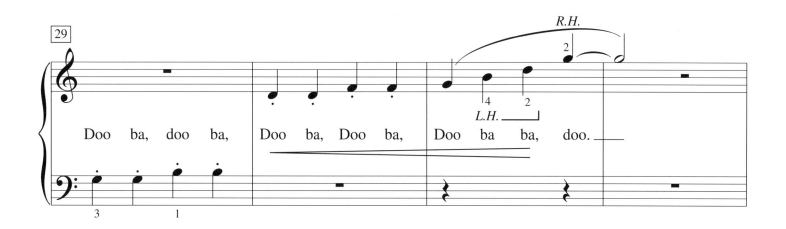

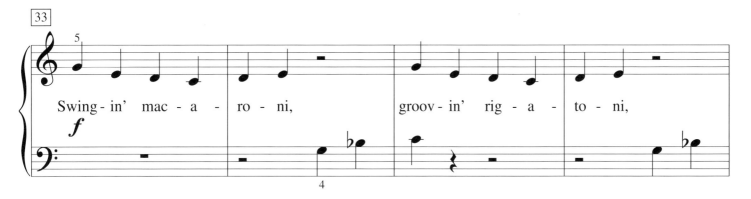

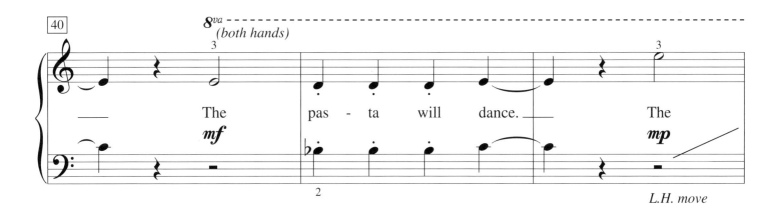

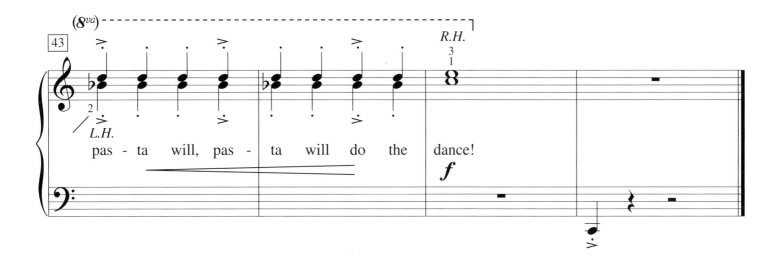

Wendy Stevens is a composer, pianist, teacher, and clinician. She received her Bachelor of Music in Piano Pedagogy and her Masters of Music in Theory and Composition from Wichita State University where she graduated *summa cum laude*. Wendy has been a recipient of the MTNA stAR award (Student Achievement Recognition Award). She has also taught theory at Wichita State University and adjudicates for music events in her area. In addition to her studio teaching, she has served as a church musician playing the piano for more than 20 years.

Wendy is a member of MTNA, KMTA, and her local association WMMTA. She has served as the president of WMMTA and has also served on the board for KMTA. She is a nationally certified teacher of music and is a member of ASCAP (American Society of Composers, Authors and Publishers).

Wendy enjoys composing and presenting workshops on creativity, composition, business practices, and technology. She maintains a popular and helpful blog for piano teachers covering such topics as business issues, teaching composition, creative studio ideas, and much more at **www.ComposeCreate.com**.